*Sea, Land, Shadow*

NEW DIRECTIONS POETRY PAMPHLETS

# KAZUKO SHIRAISHI

# *Sea, Land, Shadow*

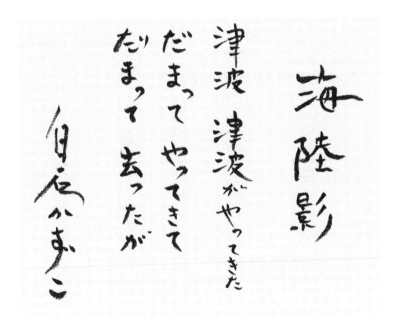

*Translated from the Japanese by*
**Yumiko Tsumura**

NEW DIRECTIONS POETRY PAMPHLET #23

Cover design by Erik Carter
Interior design by Eileen Baumgartner and Erik Rieselbach
Manufactured in the United States of America
New Directions Books are printed on acid-free paper
First published as New Directions Poetry Pamphlet #23 in 2017

*Library of Congress Cataloging-in-Publication Data*
Names: Shiraishi, Kazuko, author. | Tsumura, Yumiko, translator.
Title: Sea, land, shadow / Kazuko Shiraishi ; translated from the Japanese by Yumiko Tsumura.
Description: New York, NY : New Directions Publishing Corporation, 2017. |
Series: New Directions poetry pamphlet
Identifiers: LCCN 2017009776 | ISBN 9780811226950 (a New Directions Poetry Pamphlet :
alk. paper)
Subjects: LCSH: Shiraishi, Kazuko—Translations into English.
Classification: LCC PL861.H57 A2 2017 | DDC 895.61/5—dc23
LC record available at https://lccn.loc.gov/2017009776

10 9 8 7 6 5 4 3 2 1

ndbooks.com

New Directions Books are published for James Laughlin
by New Directions Publishing Corporation
80 Eighth Avenue, New York 10011

# Sea, Land, Shadow

## *Yellow* Waves of *Rice* Continue

what's     that *yellow* sight?
it is not flowers     it is a *yellow*     *field* of *rice*
foreigners would feel
it appears     endlessly
          the *yellow garden* is continuing
the dazzling *field* of vivid     *yellow*
continues     like a *garden*
foreigners would be *awestruck*

it is a beautiful     season of *yellow*
the undulating     *quiet* waves of *rice*     make the *field*
appear a *yellow*     luxurious
          *garden*
from there     Japanese     happiness     history
and life begins     and continues
     thank you
     *rice garden*
     the *garden* of heaven's blessing
     that makes     Japanese natural features
     beautiful     and helps the life     and
     joy     of     all Japanese

*2015*

## On a Mountain Road in a *Traffic Jam*

on a mountain road in a *traffic jam*
I have poetry, so I'm fine
             a poem is *random* and moody
always    it appears according to the mood of the moment

if I am *hungry* and mistakenly
             call for a poem, it's *no* good
the poem is moody    and *irresponsible*
             for what I wrote
but    sometimes from inside a poem
             a natural devilish
talent appears and *strides*
being *annoyed* and if I keep *making little* of it
             it's *no* good
once in a while *wisdom* like a jewel    and an unexpected
             *uncouth* future appears

intently    being patient
      I will *look*
         and *see through*
            what the *thing* called "future" will do
if it gets nowhere, *discard*
        and find a new *one*
like some *fellow*
       looking for a mistress

*2015*

## Mommy's Acquaintance, a 90-Year-Old Tree

after a long time    I have come from Tokyo
to the land with the *grapevine* trellis

here I said to Nobu, "once that tree was 90 years old,
the same *age* as my Mommy"
the old *grape* tree is the same 90 years old as Mommy
I wonder after how many years, how many decades
    have I come here
now    Mommy    no longer comes to this mountain
she is talking with eternity in sleep    in the country of sleep
eternity is talking in whispers with Mommy
and, uh    then, um    the story continues
setting out for home crossing many    mountain roads by car
the longer the road the more *relieved* I am
mountains on both sides
even an unusual tunnel
        a little *mischievous child*

*2015*

## The Sea Is Barking

waves     are rough
                    and torment me

my hair     as if in the way
keeps bothering me
even though the waves are not having sex with me
I might want to do something with you but
the wind     is rough
the sound of waves     is rough
                    and so refreshing
that I feel like playing together with you
but     you     are rough
so     I cannot swim with you     now
if you wait for me     until summer
I might play with you

the waves of the brave     rough sea     are like a brave man
and I would like to play with     you

but     it is not a man but a wave     so if I get in
it will be cold     and I will die     *sorry*
                    we cannot play
                          together     together with you
the rough waves
like a brave man     though it's been a short time
I am happy to have met you
                          something brave     like you
                          in one moment of life

soon    I have to say *goodbye* to you
and I wish you a safe    eternity
    thank you    you are a good man
in the name of waves    a refreshing
    great guy

*2015*

## Now, the Sun Is About to Hide in the Mountains

"it's OK
　　　　　as I will rise again tomorrow"
　　you don't have to make an excuse
I　　like you as you are now

leaning toward the West　　why is
the large　　*eyeball*　　staring at me
so much shining
glaring　　with a warm　　passionate eye
if you are about to set　　quietly
you could pretend but
why　　you let　　me　　know
I guess you *don't like*
*goodbyes*　　or small　　partings
so you want to kiss
our globe all over
until its *cheeks* turn red

*2015*

## Crossing Through

I think of tomorrow
"I want to cross through    you"
by you I mean tomorrow
as long as I am talking to harmless    you

but    uncrossable    tomorrow
various    uncrossables    stride
nevertheless    tomorrow    comes to ask
"when    are you going to    cross through?"

carrying a mountain of    that kind of    tomorrow
I manage to    soothe today    and let myself pass it

but    when I sleep and get up in the morning as though to
    say "Hi"
tomorrow    is waiting with a wink at me
I have no choice    saying "I will be with you"
I kiss tomorrow    "you are a good guy"
since tomorrow becomes today    the feast of
    "crossing through"
I can meet the severe pleasure

*2014*

## Falling Off the Globe

(1)

*don't go* walking that far
as you will fall off the globe

*don't* cut trees in the woods
what can you see beyond that
you can see a *naked* globe
from the globe
        even trees will end up falling

one day I took a walk with a dog
I wanted to *piddle* but the sea was *scary*
and the dog too was *scared* of such a place
but I felt there is
        a place the globe drops off
beyond the sea
the dog too seemed to have said it's *scary*
I got back near my house again
and by the *piddling* dog, I too felt *relieved*

(2)

I didn't want to fall off the globe
I went walking while thinking
I don't want to go walking that far
but after going as far as the *edge*
        I got *scared*

it's a pity that I have to say *goodbye* to the globe
the globe too, silently, intently,

                                  stares my way
you aren't really thinking
        it's right for me to part from you now


at this point, leaving there I decided to sleep
it's *scary*    so tonight too
I want to sleep on the warm *futon* of the globe
my *futon* at home is like a mother
                            hanging over the globe
tonight too the *futon* said    go to sleep
in my sleep I thought
the globe is watching over me and smiling
in the *abyss* of my dream


                                          *2014*

## Sleeping Bird

I am not sleeping     but
inside me     that bird is making a noise
the name of the bird is     Sleeping Bird
why are you trying to make me sleep?
the bird tells me  "be quiet"
and     skillfully takes
          me to the country of sleep
I     do not sleep     but
the bird     as though he is my master
orders me     "you     go to sleep"
I start sleeping like a baby
rapidly pushing through the waves of memories     then
as far as to Keefer Street, Vancouver
I arrive     there Muriel is waiting
she looks seven years old still     or three years old
but her English is perfect     and by her side
     sits Mrs. Green     at that moment
I wake up     why?     that place?     how many
tens of years ago?

*2014*

## *Mischievous* God's Birthday

why are they shining     *brilliantly*
in     the winter light
withered leaves appear     delighted
having a party     spirits high
even in winter, light is     sweet
it comes beside the *leaves*
     together     they dance
*whoosh     whoosh*
     even wind blows
*sparkle     sparkle     whizz     whizz*
light *rays* are     dazzling
                    to blinking eyes
*leaves* laugh     trees are     happy
pat     puffy     stomachs
*brilliant*     winter light is     like
a winter god     the *mischievous* god's birthday


*2014*

## Sea, Land, Shadow

sea, land, shadow, Iwanuma
the tsunami     tsunami came
in silence it came
in silence it left
this is Iwanuma

what I saw
what I met was
beyond those people     those endearing people's
souls     the souls' destination
there were no houses but a place where houses had been
at the far seashore
there was only one boat
it was a shadow
(it was a disheartened     lonely boat
of ghosts     with no one on board)

on this side there was no one
after the tsunami left
the boat alone remained
people left     disappeared
in this world no one     the boat stubbornly alone
   obstinately
people gather
the surviving relatives now
stand at the back gate of the ruins of a house
the house, maybe because it was silent     around the corner
death proudly     paying no attention
like courage     quite indifferently
floated the spirits of the dead     like ping-pong balls

the people, the boats completely gone with the tsunami
tonight you would not be able to sleep
that boat is coming
after the people all    gone
to the country of the dead
what are you going to do
tonight you would not be able to sleep

that boat is coming
this land the tsunami controls by great force
kicking all    the people    the houses    the lives
quite indifferently
only a little    cold sign of spring
pretending not to know
begins to open cherry blossoms a little
between the mountains    pretending not to notice

but
there was a man who was born in this land
he visited for the first time    in over sixty years
the memories of
his grandfather, grandmother, and childhood
might be unconsciously inspiring him to wish
somewhere the spirits exist
and talk to him tenderly
I can hear
the small voices of the spirits just born
"mommy, milk"
the big sound of a wave
it is a signal from the previous life
everyone    watch out
for the wave    don't let your guard down

the laughing of a baby
    the mother drawing the baby to her breast
    why   why   what?
what is that earth tremor   why    the earth is sinking
*bam!* a wave higher than heaven comes surging

the souls ascend to heaven
mother, father, you
everyone was by the sea wave's    thick walls,
swallowed
and shut in
their lives in an instant . . .
no one taught me
about the waves that reach heaven
higher than the houses and the woods
I can see
the houses and the boat packed in a box of
thick rough waves
no longer human beings
even the souls they had at the end
left from their bodies, and float
on the waves passing sea
and ascending to heaven
I heard the souls fly off
rising from the bodies that had lost life

the day after the tsunami there were some people who
  visited this land
already that place was a bright field
the boat as though not even a soul remained
everything with different faces
leaning on the woods    as though

it were a field of somewhere else
distant travelers from somewhere
who do not know the spirits of Iwanuma
appeared    and were looking at
all the fields of lost rice and crops in the sun
"In Iwanuma I was    born
when I was little    I left this land
and went to a far place    and have come here today"

every house was broken    or fell to pieces
at a barely standing    small yellow house in the evening
friends of the people who had lived there gathered
I could see the souls of
the people who had lived there shine
it was the boat drying its body in the dark
I saw a newspaper of the early Showa spread out
there were riddles for the dead    and for the living
but I could feel the souls were there
both deeply    filled with love
when a little warm setting sun appeared
the nearby mountain cherry trees too
have begun to bloom as if struck

goodbye
I will come to see you again

on the clouds of the souls'
deep spirits
the setting sun was reflecting

*2011*

## The Running of the Full Moon

the full moon      taking two stars      in a big hurry
rapidly      leaving clouds behind
was running
I wonder why      such      a hurry
it is not chasing something
neither is it being chased

last night I saw
while looking at the sky
the full moon      taking two stars      running away
dark velvet with two diamond buttons
and the dazzle of a perfect round
winter moon is      special      like a polished mirror
it reflects a cold      frozen      human cheek
looking cold-hearted      or generous
either because I am      lonesome      and forlorn or
I am big hearted      and in a pleasant mood

I saw the full moon      running
taking two stars      in a big hurry
rapidly      leaving clouds behind
it is      a fleeting moment but
it already has become an eternity      inside my eyes

*2004*

## Roman Condom

some people swim to this country shaped like a long boot
at the risk of their lives     Ms. J says
at a street corner     drinking a café latte
at the Roma Poesia     an African poet shouts
if you are so afraid of AIDS     why don't you put
an extra large condom     on the screen
on the microphone and on my body too     outside
an era passes by with raised voices     will, action and passion,
they became a wave of several hundred, an anti-war crowd
and fill up from path to path     from street to street
the spirits of several hundred     several thousand years ago
stand up     from the cobblestone streets slowly
   rubbing their eyes
even now their hearts have the same color
their temperature is red     their hearts are green
love and death are acute like a fighting bull's horns
those who tremble between god and devil,
which side do you take?
do you put on a condom?     or     in any country
(this long boot-shaped one too)     just the right size
security     does not exist anymore wherever on earth
   you look
not an old sorceress
but a robot comes
carrying a poison bomb from the sky
a baby sound asleep
a holiday in Rome was sucked up
through a straw in an instant
into the Audrey Hepburn movie

*2004*

## The Day I Heard the Song of the Honey Bee, Whale, and Angel

yesterday, with angel's wings
a sailing ship flew    over the sky    a white cloud
I thought    maybe a white bird    but then
it was a sailing ship    the captain looked at me    and smiled
what's the matter?    he asked me    like a professor
glaring through his glasses
I don't know what to do with tomorrow    what is it that's
  called new
what would be the best way    to deal with    the future
I can hear bass and piano
Dave and Milcho are playing*
like music    like a whisper of a honey bee
like a whale's    sweet soprano
I wonder how a beautiful    tomorrow will be born
while I closed my eyelids for a moment
both the flying sailboat    with wings
and the smiling face of the captain    have disappeared
the rest is    the shining persistence of vision    like a
  white cloud
I think    I heard the answer
from the wind telling me that I should consult a honey bee
  or a whale
Milcho    can go back to his country Bulgaria anytime
but he says    it doesn't matter where it is    as long as it's
  somewhere in the world

-------------------

* Dave Holland: jazz bassist; Milcho Leviev: jazz pianist.

and while Dave silently plays bass
I put my poem into my mouth   like a piece of candy

*2004*

## Yellow Sand

*from the day Genghis Khan ran*
*the yellow sand has been falling*
　　　　　　　　—Akito Arima

the man who wrote a *haiku*
was meeting a phantom Genghis Khan
the man called the ancient blue lion
in the continent of blowing yellow sands

that day
yellow sand blew over the Musashino plains too
the dromedary camel
who was raised in the blowing yellow sands of the Sahara
　　and called "the lion's mane" for five thousand years

he renounced the world　　and has lived alone in a cramped
　　enclosure in a zoo
without even being able to become a priest　　sitting in silence
　　for over ten years
but the yellow sands bear the smell of mother and
　　father, comrades, and an auditory hallucination of the
　　family's shouts, missed for a long time
he opens his heavy eyelids　　violently shaking his entire
　　body
giving a grunt as though going mad　　in the small
　　enclosure
he runs around　　raising clouds of dust

but ah, what he can see is only an eternity
the lonely peak of the dromedary camel
runs    beyond the ends of the earth    through time


*2004*

# To a Rainbow

*dedicated to haiku poet Niji Fuyuno*

at first a rainbow appeared
and let me know that there is a paradise on earth
that good-spirited flowers live quietly
a beautiful rainbow person with long hair
calls herself a winter field for some reason
she wore a self-woven rainbow
that appears in spring    summer    and autumn
but not in winter
to exist is a rainbow    no explanation there
therefore    she was truly    a rainbow

a few days ago I met her in Kamakura in the spring
she smiled like an early white flower
and dropped many words like a bird
into India tea    not talking about many things
made her prolific
spring, summer, autumn and even winter is warm
she kept the season in her heart-basket
on a day near Easter    she silently ascended to heaven    now
a woman who was a rainbow of this world even in winter
suddenly in heaven
people were choked with tears of light    her rainbow
woven with a celebration of life    her warm soul
couldn't help accepting even sadness and suffering

Easter day will clear up    people missing
the rainbow person, keeping love and loneliness

in their heart-baskets will wait for
    a ray of light and a smile to come down
        it is a never disappearing rainbow
        between this fleeting world and eternity


*2004*

## Journal, from Rome to a Cave

X Month X Day 2001
The end of September, poems swam to Rome. Poems flew
down from the sky. Poems came crawling on the earth. The
poems were naked, defenseless. They raised their voices and
jumped like babies. Then performers said we were poems
too, and stamped noisily on the head of Orpheus (a last will
and testament).
There is something that, conversely, springs back to life when
it is stamped on.

X Month X Day
Losego with fast talk blames and rebukes the war lovers.
And also AIDS. If you are so afraid that we have HIV, you'd
better put condoms on the poems on the big screen behind
the stage, on the microphone, and on me too.
Condom, corn, dome. Dome, corn that waves in the world,
from far away, a young man (tousled black hair and beard),
from several thousand years ago, floating down a river on a
raft, rubbed poetry all over his body, wetting his soul in the
sun, shaking tears and pleasure like a puppy.
In Italy, Visconti, Fellini, Paganini aren't alive now but not a
bit has changed. The heart, sensitive and yet ripens easily and
reddens like a tomato, the heartstrings that cannot sit still for
both love and hatred, Ms. J says "there are some who come
swimming," her love that grew in Firenze became a sweet
sun and opened its eyes wide.

everyone died    friends died    friends' friends died    those
people who were over there    and a different over there too

have begun to fill with more death    hunger and cold and
bullets and death    people who are not dead wanting to have
water and eat the red of a tomato go in and out of Lawsons
we are not directly involved so tonight let's have sex and get
married    but two million people died    from AIDS    over
there two million people out of twenty-two million have
disappeared    a seventy-two-year-old woman    lost eleven
sons to AIDS    and takes care of twenty-five grandchildren
there is nothing but soil there    scarcely any food

who is the old man with a black dog    who is the young man
who is lovesick wanting to sleep with his older brother's wife
the dream of the man who is going to become the husband
of a different woman    discarding his current wife    has
broken down to a one-legged existence    who is the old man
with the black dog    why has he shaved off his beard    many
inscrutable things happen in a Megalopolis    but everyone
watches in silence because it's a movie    I wonder where that
puppy has gone    even if it is found    one leg of the young
woman    will not grow back    severed dreams    are like a
gangrene leg cut off
they will not grow back
good night    Lolo    I'll write tomorrow

X Month X Day
about the mysticism of several hundred years ago
Tetsutaro told me
those women    were practicing the mystery in illusion
close to God and Christ    the white    river of dream    of
ecstasy! the mystery    I practiced    with a Doberman
the other day    forced its way into my ecstasy    and
illusion

even after I parted    from the Doberman    inside me
I am not sure   if that is    reality    or illusion
when one    is stared at    straight
by an almost vulgar
and yet noble beast    human beings    easily    fall off
from the magnetic field
from human being to mystery to Doberman becomes
Doberman to reality to human being
a Doberman is direct and does not have a world    but
human beings have    moreover they put mystery, illusion,
and dreams    on top of the body of soul like clothing
"go to a cave    discard all these disguises and be pure"
I hear the voice of god from the dog


*2003*

## A Vernal Planet

*dedicated to Yukio Mishima*

from the sky    a vernal planet is descending
in the figure of a boy    almost naked
emerges    from a beach
an illusion of a rainbow

mother and father and grandmother    are all far away
*whooo*    is the one hiding in the leaves?
do you know the old word—fornication?

the island of the sound of the waves    rapidly becoming
a distant view
I go to New York    and look at the journal

there is YM of several years ago    several tens of years
he is himself    of course    writing conscious of readers
tuxedo and body    kendo and theater going    because of
his impeccable aesthetics    he makes seemingly carefree
aesthetics coexist    making a brilliant person a genius    no
he is a genius by nature    he was a myth    this myth had to
come to a conclusion

whether you die    cutting your neck    or cutting your penis
dying is the same    said the woman with her angry hair erect
making her horse run
Musashino is    purple    hallelujah
and is golden    sunset
the poet who wrote in "autumn of sacred lust"    now after

thirty years has passed    once more
chants a prayer to the planet

from the sky    a vernal planet is descending
from there    he hops off and
in the same way as when he was alive
rapidly    goes on    walking
and never turns around    and like those
young men Jean Cocteau    or Jean Marais
of Mirror country    he slips out of reality

I wonder what blood tastes like    the washhouse on Lorca's
tongue    there women line up and sing in unison
MI, SHI, MA, MI, SHI, MA

time is muddled    history more than that
with its skirt pulled off    front and back mixed up
sometimes    backward    backward
marches    otherwise it does not do such things as
spilling the blood-soup of mass murder    from the future to
the past, and causing a great flood

I feed the twins of literature and art
that wink with their right eye    and hate with the left eye
delicate foods to fill their stomachs
and walk with them    the floorboards
gradually break apart    and from there
maniac ghosts    wander the infinite space of darkness
galactic    cruel, dazzling,
somehow for no reason    keep executing capital punishment
become a bundle of light
here    and there    sway in wandering

then    went toward the seashore
then    toward the seashore
taking what is called sea, in the mouth and with a belt
pliantly   and pliantly   the memory is lost

that is Rimbaud climbing this way up a sand slope
Arthur Rimbaud   that young,
as he came closer he aged, moreover, died, after he expired
cheerfully becoming an illusion and comes this way,
to meet  MI, SHI, MA   that face
further becomes a close-up,   and now
to the lips, of a face on a large screen,   into the gigantically
opened inside,
M, I,'s torso is gently taken   it is   a shark's lullaby
no   a shark has no lullaby   has only
fierce longing for   ecstasy, an aphrodisiac
Rimbaud for one second   hesitated, and on purpose
fluttered *the nobility of misery*   in Lion's wind that blows
through the desert
and suddenly let go of the thing he was holding in his mouth
Rimbaud covered his back with crocodile skin
not to show his shameful back to be deserted by the muse in
his youth and around that time
went to hide himself in a thicket of papyrus

taking no notice
M accurately turns his own revolving door   and opens it
to the Germanic world of the man who explains by means of
pictures   about political perversion, and sexual perversion
just then   Visconti   invites a lonely beautiful boy with glass
eyes whom he has hidden on the other side of the curtain
and presents in front of M

Helmut Berger sitting on a chair acting as a stripper in female
dress, the Germanic grotesque and brutality of Wagnerian
taste, sex festival with unsparing praise for the body,
purge of blood, and then a respectable looking oriental
man    calls it "a beauty filled with hatred" and leaves.
the dismal lyricism of the Nazis days,
might have flowed into    his brain as blood

Latin is better    than that    a bullfight too
look at the sky    the cheerful gypsies    look up
Chagall comes flying holding a bride even from Russia
inside this rhythm    can the warrior's way    meditate
what about    Spanish style    warrior's way
can the hair on the chest    and steak    be friends
when family with lawn    and wife    baking bread in a jewel
box called routine
he makes the hooves of a horse, a pen called creativity
run to the woods of fiction
I can see a man crying    whispering    far away
literature that ejaculates toward heaven
covering up with a white body blanket    that has the smell
of a woman
grows like mushrooms in places with many swamps    and
marshlands    and grows thick    and soon begins to walk
then people    laugh and die one by one    lyricism is
a happy thing    because it is a giant mist
that carries sorrow and despair deep in its arms

from deep inside of tatami mats    his dead grandmother calls
it is dangerous    don't go    upstairs

because he was bound by a spell he could not grow up
permanently    he had karma that compelled him to keep
growing up    permanently?    no, something
that is neither resistance nor will nor pleasure
carrying ecstasy of a difficult task, many hundreds of pages
by pen on the way running like a horse at full speed    he
stops by
at a theater or café    we call it    an interval
sometimes call it    a devil
an interval is    for him to meet the Gods
the Gods are    indecent    and were planting the ugliness of
his soul    on top of the beautiful body with desire and vanity,
and lovable honesty
even after going around the earth    Gods
are noisy    and when they see M, they beckon


and show posed muscle-bound bodies one after another
each one    laughs showing white teeth
these body-builders also walk    and    dance
and show off jumping


the Gods show trivial frogs too    and lined up pigs
in tuxedos    are raising frogs    saying that this is confidential
Miodrag Bulatovic told a story about
the men in a freight car    before they noticed
were put into a concentration camp    made into pigs by plastic
surgery    also about a man who escaped    barely    from there


on the bridge over the Danube a thousand toes lined up
corpses in red blood drifted under the bridge    and in the sky
missiles beautifully exploded    into red flames    and the toes
enduring the weight of bodies on top of them

heard a song coming out of the lips of the faces of the upper
part of the bodies    a great chorus    and the fire    and the
river    and the corpses

what has happened after M left this world
is not my concern    because he was
faithful to    fresh ideals and aesthetics
he knew what is called life    as time passes    like
persimmons ripen    get rotten    and then    wither
and drop like camellias one by one

and that is    ungraceful and something he cannot accept
even if now    his neck flies in the sky    and becomes
a crescent    like a sharp scythe
wind    is blowing ominously    as though stripping the globe
entirely    and ruffling up the sea    and making the land
naked    the trees do not even resist
the curse    of the evil spirits    that flutters hair black
having a masochistic pleasure    in branches and trunks being
wrenched off    by the roaring wind
the young man who indulged in mother's love in Visconti's
movie saying    mother    will you dance with me
tonight he whips a woman, mother white-plastered naked in
a slip    and stares at her gasping out of fear, and then blows
on the flute of the Nazis

in whatever way    the story will progress as long as the
author exists    as long as the director exists the image moves,
but one day, the author cut off his time, and leaves

the wind    seems to have stopped
soon    we will move into the next century

do you remember    we played the game of monkey's planet
thirty some years ago    on the starlit balcony
like    a star falls
a human being falls sometimes
a human voice    becomes a rainbow sometimes
there is a ritual of    holding hands up    getting on a horse
as though entering the shore of the waves of life    and disap-
pearing it is
a happening of making time flow backward    like    a boy
the fresh    sound of waves is heard    and something is born
it is    not a human being
but a story    a horse called literature
pricks up its ears    and on that current    the horse
gives a neigh    one voice    a silent
indescribable voice    that flows    between the author's
consciousness    and unconsciousness
and kicks them off    and to the next line
starts running    quietly    exquisitely    devilishly
embraced    and seduced    by both    heaven's
God    and    hell's devil
but    the horse without slowing down    conscientiously
shakes off    the author    and starts running
into infinite space

(from here return to the opening scene)

from the sky    a vernal planet is descending
in the figure of a boy    almost naked
emerges    from a beach
an illusion of a rainbow

*2003*

## The Bird Who Speaks Chuvash


a poet rode over on the Eurasian wind    the other day
because he was prohibited from publishing his poems
in the Russian language    for thirty years
he has become this kind of poet
he tried to talk about "a poem of silence"
he spoke in Chuvash
that there is a poem in this world that appears
in a place where one cannot hear even a word
silence not chattering
music without sound
paintings to see with eyes closed
Chuvash language    beside my ears
undulated    and chirped    like a bird    and then
making the branches he went to pick up    from the knees
  of gods
into a lullaby    he was putting the baby bird to sleep
that night    the Eurasian wind    throughout the night
blew    over my dreams
so inside the *futon*    in the land twenty degrees below zero
I was bathed    as though in steam
in the warm spell of a shaman


*2000*

## Go Through    Or Bar the Way


I wonder if it is safe to go through
saying go through    go through    there are land mines
snipers    also    before I know it
the bombardments from that way    and from this way
from who to whom    whose command    who is the enemy?
I had lived in Sarajevo always    my father is Croatian
my mother is Serbian    so if the Croatians and the Serbians
fight against each other    what am I supposed to do?
not only was I a good friend with a Muslim child    and we
were peaceful and happy    until a bullet came from the
outside
but now
the way is barred    the way is barred
do not go that way    do not go this way    if you go this way,
you will die    you will starve    you will burn even a bench
no more firewood to keep warm    because there was no
food both my aunt and uncle died    I was told that I am an
orphan in a refugee camp    what's happening where    not
even a telephone call comes through here    it is as if I am in
a cellar    deaf and blind    we don't have any outside infor-
mation    the people living outside in the safe zone do not
know    such things as our life and heart living in this town
(are the politicians of the world powers Gods, the war loving
  Mars? or Gods of peace)
go through    we will kill you
or barring the way    confinement    barring the way    and
then what?


*2000*


41

## A Spell of Dry Weather

the Indonesian Toufiq said
because of a spell of dry weather
the rumbling of thunder on the stone mountain
resonates even to ears that cannot hear
I asked him again     as I
cannot hear     anything     what does he mean
he said     a tear becomes a stone
I did not see     the scenery
why a small amount of tear-water becomes a stone
and many pile up     to become not a stone
but a mountain of stone
Toufiq     not only able to see it     is living inside it
when there is a s p e l l   o f   d r y   w e a t h e r     people's
t e a r s   become hard stones
and become a mountain of stone in the twinkling of an eye
by the way     from that country     Toufiq visited here
and a little while ago     he was walking alone on a morning
beach with waves crashing
taking along     one     phantom

*2000*

## A Person Dies

a person dies
who died?
my mother died
Ikuya said

a dog cries at the back    says I am hungry
a man cries at the front    says I do not want to part
but    in April the cherry blossoms
snow    *suddenly*    falls
a person dies
one person parts from another person

Kaoru says
p l e a s e
the beer she bought for us
filled with    scattered golden tears
how    merry
tonight's    vigil is

then after a meal
we went out to dance
men were getting drunk from the lower half of the body
but    I do not get drunk
between the drunk lower half of my body    and the not
drunk upper half of my body
I listen to Otis
the dead do not get drunk
to watch    a person dying
one does not get drunk either

but     a dog is different
when it says I am hungry
I will give it     ample food
also     to a living human being
I do not give food in a half-hearted way
but when a person dies
I will offer     a little
a token of condolence money
counting what I have in my wallet
and keeping some for tonight's meal

a person dies
it is April so
in the kitchen     the smell of boiling new potatoes
the green flame     of the spinach
the appetite vigorously and quietly growing
the desire for sex
and     a person dies     really
Ikuya's     mother     completely
has disappeared

*1994*

44

## A Requiem for the Earth

one who dies does not return to life
so we make a memorial day call to the dead person
Issui Yoshida, Samantha, and Teruo's father
all have died
riding on a swan    on a drug    on a glow in the morning sky
each had a different style
but set out on a journey
"write down the memorial day, your own memorial day"
even though you aren't dead yet
even though you're still alive
for the sake of your own self that will die    in advance
write a memorial day poem    a requiem
Gozo says
Gozo too is alive
and I am alive too
the others my friends    and their surroundings too
though not quite satisfactory    the earth is still
alive    during the time I am alive
a new star is born    and disappears
toward a black hole
I will send a requiem for my
living being

a poem in the middle of my life
not yet dead but alive    putting down
the land that has still    ample green
the air that is dirty    but has a sweet life
the ear of a twenty-year-old sailor who will set sail
the black sound that perches    there
with dripping sweat Stevie's blind    rainbow voice    inside

to each one of those
before they leave the earth
one should send
a salutation
poem of soul pacifying    a charm for the memorial day

the soul of Miss A says
getting up from the coffin
"Ah, before I noticed    I've been dead"
to this soul    I put on a record of
Mary Wells but
to the soul of this bank of the living
now    I turn on the music of
Earth, Wind & Fire
the ones who are alive too
death has begun    while being alive
while harmonizing with    fighting    hating
and loving    death that has begun
heads for the beach of the end but

now
I can see
many thousands    many tens of thousands of globes
go flying
with frightening speed
toward the cemetery that was dug at the end of the universe
the giant throat of the black hole
the rearview mirror of my thoughts is
a lonely planetarium    multimillion years ahead
I can see there    in the future
the death not yet    reached death doing a trial run for
   death

and the death that falls    pouring chaotic energy
and the sacred life's march in the desert of quiet    life
it is not that everything    has died out
they are on the side of the living now
I can see even though this is not hell
the memorial days that hatch in the days of the living
the cemetery that swells daily
I can hear    because this is hell

I shall send a requiem
at first
to the earth in the future    gradually    getting worn out
and heading for death
if a living person    to oneself
gives water while being alive
gives flowers while being alive
gives words    prayer
and love while being alive

I can hear my voice of a thousand years later
tomorrow is
my memorial day
it seems to be    my memorial day

*1994*

## Santa Barbara—Newly Wed and Nearly Dead

Kenneth* said
gods    do not exist
he cannot hear voices
from anywhere    or anything
a young nurse seemed to have asked him
if he can see    some
future    beyond death

death
from the side of the mountain of the highest wisdom
  of the brain

is disappearing
at a brisk pace    to the ocean's skirt
with the foam of many marriages

*1984*

---

* Kenneth Rexroth (1905–1982) died in Santa Barbara, California, and is buried there on
  a cliff by the sea.

## Ear

pretending to hear    nothing
her earlobe    is sleeping
all the world is
far away now
it does not reach    as far as her ear

a thin fairy of
pleasure    parched like a honey bee
on the woman's earlobe    sometimes
completely    stops hearing sounds
suddenly
captured by    a thick lip
she squirms in a sea of torture    of cruel teeth
with a shiver of the thin fairy
the woman    gradually    throughout her body
becomes a lively bell of the woods    and rapidly
recovers the world    inside

*1984*

## Window of an Eye

today I can see the sky     from the window
of your eye
you
are a cheerful blue
you lean out toward me
from the window of your eye
and are about to drop
firmly     and embrace me
in the depth of     the window of your eye
now     you try to rub your cheek on mine
so     in a fluster
I close the curtain of my eyelashes
you close your window
and the music of     a blink
with extreme     swiftness
passes     stroking
my soul


*1984*

## The Palm of the Hand

The palm of his hand
was a big room
a map of various fates    written there
a vast    warm
world

being veiled in
the palm of that man's hand
I cannot see
myself any longer

in parting from the palm of his hand
I    am suddenly
a drifting star with its thread cut
sliding away    down the outside    of the world

*1984*

## In September

a moon appeared
a moon appeared over the grass-covered plain
I want to give you
one delicious full moon
like romantic love

I want to drink a full moon
floating it in a saké cup
I drink the full moon     with delicious saké
and store it away     somewhere in my heart
pretending nothing happened

that kind of full moon
that kind of love     in September
one for you     one for me
I want to try eating it like a dumpling

*1984*

## March or an Aperitif

there is a vast hill
and there is sky beyond the hill
but always the other side is not visible
so I cannot help thinking there will be some future

spring    is right near me    but I cannot touch it
like my love expected to come

March is    the season I look forward to
if applied to drinking    it is an aperitif
wondering what feast    what romance
what drama    will follow    next
the buds of the pussy willow swell
the wind is still winter's but    the air begins
to bear a sweet fragrance

*1984*

## The Man with Fiery Eyes

he has fire    in his eyes
when stared at    firmly    I get hot
even a cold heart    and chilled stomach
are warmed up
he    has the African sun in his eyes
a man with the pride of the Zulu royal family
on a break from the revolution
the meat he roasted for me
in the oven was so delicious
in the living room    his one-year-old twins La and Re
took turns crying
the fiery eyes    gently    caressing them
sang a lullaby
there was    a moment    warm
earth    warmed and became happy from the core
in the living room of the man with fiery eyes


*1984*

## Lizard God or Urururu

what is trembling isn't a flower    but me
I am a spirit called lizard    a living creature born fifty
thousand years ago
now    a wind passes over me    carrying voices
it resembles the sound of a propeller
it reaches my ears    from the direction of the future universe
it reaches me    very close by
toward the red    orange    yellow    light purple
rock I am sitting on
what they came to convey to me
the voices    the quivering
    that beautiful music
    the mating stars
    the sexual intercourse of the star people
I hear the voice of a praying person inside me
I hear the voice of a laughing and whispering person
he is a young aborigine who just turned twenty-seven
now    he sits on top of Urururu    the rock mountain in
the central desert of a continent    of the southern hemisphere
of the planet called Earth
and he is playing a didgeridoo
it is the tone of a beautiful look and resolve
the didgeridoo is an admonition to mankind
that inclines toward Noah's ark bound for a twenty-first-
    century star
it is a signal to the quivering
spirit    that still    sometimes    inhabits
this place    the star called Earth
the quiver    finds its way inside me

from fifty thousand years ago to fifty thousand years in
    the future
the quiver    the ones that quiver    the spirit or
the mating stars    star people
listen!
now    on the rock mountain of Urururu a young man
is playing a didgeridoo
I could hear urururu    urururu
listening to the sound
I    don't tremble
I and the flower and the lizard    all quiver
through the quiver toward the future
I go to meet
the mysterious voices that resemble the sound of a propeller
together with a young aborigine
together with the internal lizard god
together with
the internal
lizard god

*1983*

# Vulture

the Jamaican man
has the eyes of a robber
has the sharp     clear
eyes     of a vulture

when he thinks of
his brother     who was born
mentally disabled     turning twelve
always sleeping
lying in a hospital bed
this     life
which knows nothing but sleep
when he thinks while looking far
the Jamaican man is
no longer     a robber
he has clear
sad eyes
as noble as
a pure     beast
he is that     other vulture
perching
glancing over     far away
in the shade of rocks     without
even the shadow     of a tall tree

*1970*

## The Pithecanthropus Erectus's Hobby


the Pithecanthropus Erectus has a hobby too
he is raising me

for a few weeks he gave me old-fashioned food
and has been teaching me such sports as
sexual intercourse
loving
and biting an enemy to death

I am being tamed little by little
and forgetting my own language    my face disappearing
the Pithecanthropus Erectus    now
is raising a strange me that I don't recognize    anymore

the bones remaining white on the hill after I am chewed to
    death
without knowing at all it is me    I am now
cheerfully    barking
I continue to live on


*1970*

## October Sentimental Journey

you are the October moon
that full moon without a face    when
open-hearted laughter arrives
along the twilight way
your youth    suddenly    ages
sentimental journey
your love    opens its mouth like a crocodile
and now    brushes its teeth
and on those white teeth
your days    small lies
become small truths
both well nourished
perch in lustrous happy light

even with your large eyes
you cannot see    the melody of "Sentimental Journey"
the song floating from this boundless October

but
you will hear
the wooden horse's tail    go round
and round with pleasure    like a merry-go-round
resembling the bravery of your tail
everything    and the merry-go-round
are rotating phantoms

but
both you    and I
do not go round and round

just     pass by
in a smart-looking     manner
a cloud crossing the full moon
ah, October moon
there is a full moon without a face
existence without a name
you     exist

*1968*

## Bye Bye Blackbird

Bye Bye Blackbird
it is not that
several hundred birds     several thousand birds fly away
always what flies away is one bird
from inside me
dangling my ugly internal organs
every time I get pregnant with you
I lose my sight     inside blindness
I live sniffing the world
when I lose you     I see you for the first time
but at that moment     my up to now presence dies
and life in a new blindness begins to move

Bye Bye Blackbird
he sings on the stage transforming into one bird
his audience chases his bird     becoming several tens of
thousands of ears
at that time     the audience is the blind wings of several
hundred thousand
the audience who cannot see     flapping their wings
becomes a ghost of a bird
and chasing the voice of one bird on the stage
dances over the seats in the dark
but I wonder if anyone can tell     which one isn't a ghost
but a real bird     again
Bye Bye Blackbird
he who is singing cannot tell either
what is it     that truly flies away from here
only     he is singing wildly     and feels

that now in which something is flying away    is certain
it may be his velvety time
it may be the extremely soft sirloin of his soul
or it may be the star memory of his guilty crime
or it may be warm blood
that splashes from the tulip-shaped brain of a child
    sitting in the front row

Bye Bye Blackbird
I am a bird
whether I refuse myself
or accept myself
as long as I cannot snatch away
this pointed beak that doesn't stop pecking
and the wings that have a flapping habit
today    I am a bird
I become a prayer    and a bird    several times a day
piercing the sky    am thrust out of the sky    and fall
or internal organs that carry a falling bird
inside me    there are these giant birds that fall down
small birds    from a lean and old bird    to an arrogant
and sweet bird
and some are half alive and groaning
I give funerals to these birds as my daily task
on the other hand
I warm the eggs of future birds as my daily task
the stranger the bird that bites off the future, the more I love
    and desperately warm its eggs
Bye Bye Blackbird
I am thinking of becoming a strange bird
and try making the one that eats me up fly away
really I must make that one fly away    to the point blood

gushes out
elegantly    singing
Bye Bye Blackbird


*1965*

## Ulysses in Mid-Summer

I keep walking where
Nick keeps blooming
blooming like a poisonous weed
wearing almost nothing     drinking nothing
already     several days, several hours, no several years

by now Nick has grown old
it is difficult     for me     to see
the toenails of a young man's steel feet running
with a football     and his face     the stone teeth     in his
shining smiling mouth
the unruly horse called a juvenile delinquent
living in his eyes     time's chain already *killed by inches*
I     now     see the shadow of a man in his manhood
whom I don't know, called Ulysses
in a room in the sky that his eyes cannot see
on his forehead     time and various days
become sweaty     and change to clouds and birds
also     at the side of his spine     there is a slight
trace of teeth marks made by a seal of his fate
and still     wet     as though from a recent incident
instead of agile sadness
mixed with the elegance and poverty of old times
the weight of the waves of some complex flesh and soul
that goes back and forth between offshore and shore
of his muscles but
the mysterious acoustics of the sound of the waves
even he himself     often cannot hear
although a person has music inside his body
before hearing one's music

one leaves from life or
sleeps all one's life without taking notice of it

without knowing he is a Ulysses
incessantly he lives    incessantly he dies
insulting the god inside me    or
becoming a god to be insulted on my altar
the word eternity is beyond
this incessant restlessness

I    never get used to
counting his age and soul
that increases in volume    year by year
like a dog obsessed with sniffing    I always lick my lips
and loiter around the soul that resembles putrid fresh

because a person cannot
measure    a soul    with love
and count life made of a notch of time
a person is a bird possessed by
the game of continuing this work endlessly
but the soul leaves the bird behind and pushes toward infinity
and the age is a skillful fool who betrays the one who counts
the age

especially    these days
August is no longer July
the age of summer    swells up noticeably
I have a hunch of cumulonimbus
it changes suddenly from a growing lion
to the languid    immovable weight
of a pregnant lioness

inside the lazy afternoon of a lion's half-open eyes
and sometimes in the shiver of winds that cross its mustache
I hear a light tremolo of a rain cloud, time and fate that
change the sky   before I notice it
and never fail to see its shadow
and
for the sake of
the inviolable   or   the absolute
I think   about a piece on the altar
the flesh of vulgar origin   that never decomposes
as for the other's flesh
it is not that   vulgar
and not that   beautiful
and not that   ugly
I think of many tasteless tastes of time
passing through   adding spices
called special chance, goodness, love, and hatred
to say that is   that
is an enormous countless waste

when one learns that it is vulgar   in addition to being rough
and now   that it is not gold, but fake, easy to peel off
a human has the nature of a mother wolf that raises
a fake the same as a real
friendly like a twin   nonchalantly
therefore   inside love   justice is ominous
and both its edges are the thin lips
of a razor easy to betray

I keep walking
through the inside of something that keeps blooming
almost like a hunger

the shadow that keeps walking     is Ulysses
or
if not Ulysses perhaps it is fine
whether it is Nick     or him
because everything is something that does not have a name
rather
it is I     and not even I
when I keep walking
my insides     in that way
I can touch     for sure
only the sway of the wind of poisonous weeds

today I keep living
listening to
the unsorted lively chaos     of butterflies, fairies, and shells
a pupil madly collected     with obscure intentions
at the start of summer vacation     he pursued the assign-
ment too feverishly     and forgot its purpose
and the monologue     of the music
incompatible     and alienated

*1965*

# The Crocodiles

*for Nick and Muriel*

we are the savage crocodiles
that devour each other's limited time
under the severe July sun
shedding blood into a river
we cannot forget    the memory of biting
each other's life to death
like the first hatred    the first love
oh    Sun!    our godless prayer is
to beat
our actions    with one's tail
nevertheless    we
are the savage crocodiles
that devour each other's limited time
under the severe July sun

*1965*

## By the Hudson River

from whom was I born
from a bed    from a hard bed

as if a meaty bone dropped from a dog's mouth
I was dropped

my parents were round
and smooth like a moon
with human faces
and human smells

a smell of darkness
a smell of a silent woods

that's all    in New York
by the Hudson River
I am standing

I am the same as    this river
flowing

I am the same as    this river
standing

too wide to measure    the breadth of your chest
too far to measure    your memory

I don't have to go back    to the time I was born
my memory

both my destination and now    drift in my mind
even I    cannot measure

by the Hudson River
a curly-haired
black-faced child
lean with large eyes    when I

laugh    as if crying
my face breaks    and begins to shake

when I sing    I do a sinuous dance
as if the world    exists in my hips

my name is Billy
I don't know my name in the past
I don't know    the sky I was born from
what tree it was    or if I had leaves of brothers    or not
I don't know the stable    I was born in
was it a straw bed    or a wooden bed

nevertheless    I grew up
like the cheeks of a grown fruit
at the fruit shop
while I was looking at fruits I couldn't buy

at a butcher shop
while I was watching a pig leg    being cut off

by the Hudson River
I stand now    alone

carrying myself a little grown up
my grandma     grandpa
my dear love     the Hudson River

I     will go floating     with the river
with the big flowing Hudson     in my mind
with the Hudson that flows with me     in my mind

*1963*

# The Star

"Are you shy?" it asked
there is a knocking sound in the box
a breath and a breath communicate
the winter moon like a hazy moon on a spring night
ice hugged me tight
the mist got drunk and came to kiss me
I stayed still
it came to ask me again
"Are you shy?"
my eyes were heavy
and began to open toward a star

*1951*